HOUSE OF MANY TONGUES

Also by Jonathan Garfinkel:

Ambivalence: Crossing the Israel/Palestine Divide
Glass Psalms
The Trials of John Demjanjuk: A Holocaust Cabaret
Walking to Russia

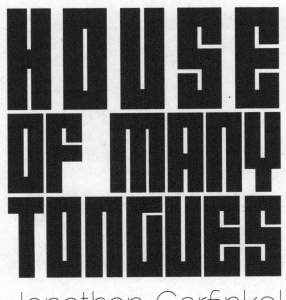

HOUSE OF MANY TONGUES

Jonathan Garfinkel

Playwrights Canada Press
Toronto

PLAYWRIGHTS CANADA PRESS
The Canadian Drama Publisher
215 Spadina Ave., Suite 230, Toronto, ON Canada M5T 2C7
phone 416.703.0013 fax 416.408.3402
info@playwrightscanada.com • www.playwrightscanada.com

For professional or amateur production rights, please contact:
Michael Petrasek of Kensington Literary Representation
34 St. Andrew Street, Toronto, ON M5T 1K6
kensingtonlit@rogers.com, phone 416.979.0187

Playwrights Canada Press acknowledges the financial support of the Government of Canada through the Canada Book Fund and the Canada Council for the Arts, and of the Province of Ontario through the Ontario Arts Council and the Ontario Media Development Corporation, for our publishing activities.

Cover art and design by Carolyn McNeillie
Type design by Blake Sproule

LIBRARY AND ARCHIVES CANADA CATALOGUING IN PUBLICATION
Garfinkel, Jonathan
House of many tongues / Jonathan Garfinkel.

A play.
Also issued in electronic formats.
ISBN 978-0-88754-960-1

I. Title.

PS8563.A646H69 2011   C812'.6   C2011-900631-6

First edition: April 2011
Printed and bound in Canada by Gauvin Press, Gatineau

Dedicated to the real Alex, four a.m. by a piano in the Basement Theatre, Tbilisi, and to Abu Dalo and Shimon, eternal neighbours.

Playwright's Note

The Israeli-Palestinian conflict is one of the last taboo subjects of our times. In North America it is a topic discussed with great difficulty and is often met with resistance, fury and disgust. "Anti-Zionist" and "anti-Semite" are but two of the slurs I had thrown at me in response to my trying to engage this theme. The political and cultural climate is one that says we must be sensitive to history, politically correct and culturally sensitive. This is a tiresome argument for any writer; it just isn't kosher to criticize Israel or Palestine these days.

That I chose to explore this subject through theatre is not a novel approach. That I attempted to do so with absurdism and magical realism has to do with the reality of the situation: I wanted to capture something of the near-mythic levels of irrational madness that possess people in laying claim to a land as their own while excluding the other. This play is anti-war—which contains its own irrationality. But it is also about the way we repeat ourselves, again and again, *ad nauseam*.

The play has seen various incarnations. In reading over the different versions leading up to this publication, I remembered a discussion with E.C. Woodley and Nikki Landau. We were watching the actors and the numerous drafts were scattered on the Tarragon stage. Opening night was approaching; there was yet another rewrite. We agreed that the scene in front of us—the countless pages, the director trying a new line, me scratching another one out—might make the most truthful version of the Israeli-Palestinian play: one that is constantly shifting, constantly arguing over right and wrong, and always failing. I hope there is something in these lines that acknowledges that mess.

Jonathan Garfinkel
Berlin, 2011

House of Many Tongues received its world premiere in German (Das Haus der vielen Zungen) at the Bochum Schauspielhaus in Bochum, Germany, in October 2008. It was translated by Frank Heibert and directed by Kristo Šagor.

A significantly revised version of the play premiered in English at the Tarragon Theatre in Toronto, Canada, on May 5, 2009. It was directed by Richard Rose and featured the following cast and crew:

Alex—Daniel Karasik
Shimon—Howard Jerome
Abu Dalo, Mahmoud Darwish—Hrant Alianak
Suha—Erin McKinnon
Rivka, Melissa's Vagina, Shabak Agent—Nikki Landau
The Camel—Raoul Bhaneja
The House—Fiona Highet

Teresa Przybylski—set and costumes
E.C. Woodley—sound design

The text in this published edition is a slightly modified version of the Tarragon production.

The Palestinians are in Palestine because they have no other place in the world. The Israeli Jews are in Israel for the same reason—they have no other place in the world.

This provides for a perfect understanding and a terrible tragedy.

—Amos Oz

If the olive trees knew the hands that planted them, their oil would become tears.

—Mahmoud Darwish

Characters in Order of Appearance:

Shimon: The General, sixty-one
Alex: Author of the *Cunnilingus Manifesto*, son of Shimon, fifteen
Rivka: The cousin and tutor of Alex, twenty-eight
Melissa's Vagina: Female
The House: Female
Abu Dalo: Displaced Palestinian, the Writer, fifty
The Camel: Male
Suha: The daughter of Abu Dalo, object of Alex's desire, fifteen
Mahmoud Darwish: Palestinian national poet, sixty
Shabak Agent: Female, thirties

Act I

Scene 1

Israel, 1988. By the Jordan River. SHIMON, in army fatigues, drinking beer.

SHIMON   We're waiting here to kill or be killed.
              Waiting for the enemy to speak its name.

              If you look to the left,
              you can see the wind blow dust around the hills.
              They say this hill is holy.
              Something or other was sacrificed here,
              someone had a vision over there.
              That's what we're killing for.
              Something so holy even the earth will bleed.

              Kill or be killed.

SHIMON washes his hands in the river. A basket floats toward him. Laughs.

              And there's the miracle. A basket. Floating on the Jordan River.

There's a bundle with a baby on it. SHIMON removes the child from the raft.

What the fuck? A baby!
Doesn't make a sound. Not a peep. Doesn't even cry. You Moses or
something?

Picks up his beer.

L'chayim Moses!
You want some, little brother?
You want a beer with me?

You're not death, little brother.
You're life. The land is your mother.
And that unknown something
that controls time and farts out our stinking fates
is your father. They gave us to each other.

Welcome to the Holy Land.
Welcome to your Home.

Scene 2

2003. A house in Jerusalem.

The bundle in the raft becomes ALEX, aged fifteen.

He holds a pen and a pad of paper. SHIMON, drinking beer, wears army fatigues.

ALEX   Dad, who's my mother?

SHIMON   The land is your mother. Are you writing this down?

            May 15, 1988. The fortieth anniversary of our nation. And the birth
            of my son.

ALEX   I don't want to write this.

SHIMON   We write our history. Together. Father and son.

ALEX   *(He puts down the pen.)* I don't want to.

SHIMON   Come on, kid. It's our story.

ALEX   I don't like this story.

SHIMON   It's your story. How you were born.

ALEX   I want to know who my real mother is.

SHIMON presents ALEX with a gun.

SHIMON   Happy fifteenth birthday, Alex.

ALEX   The gun?

SHIMON   1934 German Mauser. I fought in the '67 War with this. Defended
              and overcame with this. An entire hillside ours because of this gun.

ALEX reluctantly takes it.

ALEX   That's great, Dad.

SHIMON   It's consistency. Better than any woman you'll ever meet. Beautiful.
              Powerful. Reliable too.

ALEX   This gun is not beautiful.

SHIMON   This gun is the Miracle of '67.
              My legacy.
              From me to you.

ALEX   I don't want your gun.

SHIMON   You have to write the story of the gun.
              Our story.
              The miracle of how you were born!

ALEX   I don't want to write your book.

SHIMON   Hope was you on a river arriving into my arms.
              Hope was this house I found in the fucked-upness of war.

Hope was the birth of this nation!
Nearly sixty years ago, David Ben-Gurion had a vision for our people:
To be a light unto nations.
In one week's time, your hero Ilan Ramon will be the first Israeli to travel
into outer space. This hope will become manifest.
That's how great this country is.
We can send men to the stars!

ALEX   *(robot-like)* This is the twenty-first century. I don't believe in miracles. I don't care how great this country is.

SHIMON   Sure you do.

ALEX   I don't care about outer space.

SHIMON   To tell a story, you have to start at the beginning.
We will write the truth.

ALEX   Tell me who my mother is and I'll write your story.

SHIMON   I give you this gun and you write our story.

ALEX   Uch! *(ALEX storms out.)*

SHIMON   Help me write!
Help me be my eyes.
Happy birthday, Alexander.

Scene 3

ALEX in his room, writing.

ALEX   My dad's a liar.
Under his mattress there lives a woman named Melissa.
I found her.

Melissa's beautiful. She's glossy, folds out in three parts and comes from Ohio. She also has lemon meringue slathered permanently around her breasts. Makes her tits look like a glazed challah.

I follow her body with my eyes. Down. Down to something I've never seen before. It's mysterious and beautiful and I have an urge to do something—to make contact.

MELISSA'S VAGINA
          Liberate me, Alex.

ALEX   Oh my God... her thing... it speaks.

MELISSA'S VAGINA
          Liberate me.

ALEX   It says.

          Liberate you?

MELISSA'S VAGINA
          Take me away from him.

ALEX   It says.

          But I'm only fifteen,
          I say.

MELISSA'S VAGINA
          It's time for you to become a man.
          To travel to where no Israeli has ever gone before.
          To boldly enter the cosmos.
          Use your tongue—for a man needs to use his tongue
          so he can learn to speak
          in new ways.
          Cunnilingus.

ALEX   It says.

          Cunnilingus?
          I say.

          Enter RIVKA.

RIVKA   Happy birthday, Alex!

Radio sounds.

ALEX   Houston, this is space shuttle Columbia. We're ready for takeoff.

HOUSTON   Copy, Alex. All systems go.

ALEX   I'm heading to where no man has gone before.

HOUSTON   Roger that. You be careful in there.

ALEX   I'm staring into the cosmos, Houston. I'm ready for entry. And I'm
             terrified.

RIVKA   Did you do your homework?

ALEX   You betcha.

RIVKA   That's fantastic!

ALEX   The truth is, Rivka... May I call you Rivka?

RIVKA   You always call me Rivka.

ALEX   I like your stockings.

RIVKA   Huh?

ALEX   You're wearing very nice stockings.

RIVKA   Right.

ALEX   Your stockings look like silk. Are they?

RIVKA   Polyester.

ALEX   I imagine they're not as soft as your skin.

RIVKA   Uh-huh.

ALEX   Although it's not your skin that interests me. It's what's beneath.

RIVKA   What's beneath my skin?

ALEX   Well, you know.

RIVKA   Alex. Are you coming on to me?

ALEX   No. I'm warming up my intentions.

RIVKA   What are you talking about?

ALEX   I'm going to give you cunnilingus.

RIVKA   What?

ALEX   Teach me how.

RIVKA   No way!

ALEX   Please.

RIVKA   I'm twice your age.

ALEX   Your experience is vital.

RIVKA   I'm your tutor.

ALEX   Exactly.

RIVKA   Your math tutor. I'm also your cousin.

ALEX   It has not been proven that we are of the same blood. And besides, even if we were. Isn't it always better to keep things in the family?

RIVKA   Your dad would kill me.

ALEX   If that's the only reason why you don't want me to perform the act of cunnilingus—

RIVKA   That's enough. Your father told me you were suspended from school today.

ALEX   It's just for three days. I needed some time off anyways. I need to get to work.

RIVKA   What did you do to get suspended?

ALEX   *(ignoring her)* Why are teachers so stupid? Why can't they teach us something important, like something we might actually use in life? Something that would change the world—for good.

Scientifically he begins to move his tongue back and forth.

             Is it better to go side to side or up and down?

RIVKA   Alex, your father's worried about you.

ALEX   *(takes out pen and paper)* My father says that Israeli men don't like to perform cunnilingus. Is this true?

RIVKA   Of course not.

ALEX   *(writing)* Oh. You mean some Israeli men do perform cunnilingus?

RIVKA   Of course.

ALEX   Are they any good?

RIVKA   I don't know. I haven't let every man in Israel go down on me.

ALEX   Roughly how many would you say do it? Plus or minus three percent.

RIVKA   Alex. We are not having sex together.

ALEX   I don't want to copulate with you. I want to learn how to give you oral pleasure. Perfectly. *(a beat)* Hey. You're blushing. What are you scared of?

RIVKA   I'm not scared.

ALEX	Then you're ashamed.
RIVKA	I am not ashamed.
ALEX	When a person feels shame it's because they can't handle the truth of things. Because the truth is too much and it weighs on you like a stone. But you haven't done anything bad, Rivka. All you want is to feel good. Like any human being. And I want to help you.

He writes in his notebook.

RIVKA	What are you writing?
ALEX	*(reading)* An anonymous source said, "Older women prefer not to talk about oral sex."
RIVKA	I didn't say that. You're misquoting me.
ALEX	You've implied that by your actions.
RIVKA	What are you writing this down for?
ALEX	My social studies independent project: the *Cunnilingus Manifesto*.
RIVKA	Good God.
ALEX	My father says no Israeli men like to go down on women. I say, that's the problem right there. If Israeli men went down on Palestinian women. And Palestinian men went down on Israeli women. And if these men could put in the time, and do it well, the world would be a completely different place. I read that orgasms alter your DNA. Isn't that what we need? A radical altering of perspective?
RIVKA	Please don't tell me this is why you were kicked out of school.
ALEX	I saw the burning bush. It spoke to me!

Climbs onto his desk.

"From Jaffa to Jericho,
Eilat to Eilon,
You, Alexander, must go forth into the nation of Israel!
And you will recruit five hundred men into your legions,
and you will set forth upon the land,
and bring pleasure to the women of Palestine.
Happy and satisfied will be the women of our enemy."

RIVKA   You want sex, Alex. That's healthy. Go find someone your own age and use a condom.

ALEX   I read in Wikipedia that there's a part of the female body that exists only for the sake of pleasure. Is this true?

RIVKA   It's called the clitoris.

ALEX   That's right. *(writes)* Cli-toris. Is it hard to find?

RIVKA   For most men, yes.

ALEX   Would you show me where it is?

RIVKA   No.

ALEX   You're my tutor. I trust you. I don't trust anyone else.

RIVKA   It's not right.

ALEX   What's right, Rivka? Is war right? Is learning how to shoot a gun at your enemy right? You're going to reserve duty in a couple of weeks. Wouldn't you rather there be peace? To not have to fight?

RIVKA   Of course I want peace. Who doesn't want peace? But oral sex is not going to stop martyr wackos from blowing up innocent people.

ALEX   How do you know cunnilingus won't save the Middle East?

RIVKA affectionately touches ALEX.

RIVKA   You're sweet, Alex.

Now. Can we get to your homework?
You don't want to fall too far behind.

Scene 4

That same afternoon. SHIMON *speaks into a tape recorder. Drinking beer.*

SHIMON   Now. The General led the campaign of the '67 War into East Jerusalem. He shot whatever was in his path. He was wild and unstoppable. Did he have regrets? There was no time for regret. It was three nations against one. For six days the General protected his country. He was fearless and bold. That was his genius.

He was young.
Beautiful.
Even the killing was beautiful.
There was Dan and the General on a hill.
They were talking and laughing when a bullet went through Dan's left eye and his skull exploded like an apple.
Everything is beautiful when you are young.

Thousands of us marched into East Jerusalem, singing "Yerushalayim of Gold."
He had shivers in June.
He wept at the Wailing Wall.
The General was wounded in the left shoulder.
He wandered out of the city in a fever and followed the tracks of the old Palestine railroad.
There was no one around. It was quiet. Everyone was either celebrating or dead.
All of a sudden, he was surrounded by silence. The impossibility of space in Jerusalem. And in that space, a house. It appeared before his eyes.

TAPE   A house. It appeared before his eyes.
A house. It appeared before his eyes.

SHIMON'*s vision, 1967. Lights up on* THE HOUSE. SHIMON *is wounded.*

THE HOUSE   Hey you. Got anything to eat?

SHIMON	Are you talking to me?
THE HOUSE	No. I'm talking to the leaky faucet. Of course I'm talking to you.
SHIMON	But you're... a house.
THE HOUSE	And you're a moron. But we can still have a conversation. Amazing, isn't it? Now. What do you have to eat?
SHIMON	Nothing. I've barely eaten in days.
THE HOUSE	God. What are you good for?
SHIMON	I can fight.
THE HOUSE	That's not gonna help. Can you eat a fight? Can you sleep on a fight? What else do you got?
SHIMON	Well, it depends on what you want.
THE HOUSE	Ah. I sense a negotiation coming. I like a good negotiation. What are your terms?
SHIMON	For what?
THE HOUSE	The negotiations.
SHIMON	I don't know what we're negotiating.
THE HOUSE	We're negotiating what you're going to give me.
SHIMON	For what?
THE HOUSE	For whatever you want.
SHIMON	Well, I want to come inside.
THE HOUSE	That'll cost you.
SHIMON	How much?

THE HOUSE	That remains to be determined.
SHIMON	How do we do that?
THE HOUSE	What do you have to offer? A knife. Still sharp. Recently used. And. A '34 Mauser. Empty cartridge. Ahh… a photograph. Who's the broad?
SHIMON	My mother.
THE HOUSE	That's no good. Not at all.
SHIMON	What am I doing wrong?
THE HOUSE	You're just not the right type.
SHIMON	The right type of what?
THE HOUSE	The right type of person to live here.
SHIMON	Live here?
THE HOUSE	That's what you want, isn't it?
SHIMON	I didn't know it was available to live in.
THE HOUSE	Well there's nobody here.
SHIMON	Where'd they all go?
THE HOUSE	They just picked up and left.
SHIMON	Just like that?
THE HOUSE	Just like that.
SHIMON	So you… could be my house then?
THE HOUSE	Ah.

SHIMON	You're a Jewish house.
THE HOUSE	I speak sixty-seven different languages. Hebrew happens to be my favourite.
SHIMON	Well I need a house. I need a home.
THE HOUSE	And what do I get?
SHIMON	I promise to take care of you. To be good to you.
THE HOUSE	I'm going to need at least one child.
SHIMON	But I have none.
THE HOUSE	Then get started.
SHIMON	I have no wife.
THE HOUSE	A house demands a child.
SHIMON	And if I don't provide one?
THE HOUSE	You don't get to keep me.
SHIMON	How long do I get?
THE HOUSE	I'll give you twenty-one years.
SHIMON	That's a reasonable offer.
THE HOUSE	I'm a reasonable house. Oh yes. And when your child is old enough, it must have a child too. In this very residence.
SHIMON	Lineage.
THE HOUSE	I'm a sucker for tradition.
SHIMON	I promise. There'll be a child. There'll be life.

THE HOUSE	You'll promise in blood.

SHIMON   You are the vision of an entire nation!

THE HOUSE   Do you see the leak in my roof? It means I'm crying. I need a garden. I need paint jobs and touch-ups, the smell of cooking and good pipes—

2003. Enter ABU DALO.

ABU DALO   Hello? Hello? Is anybody here?

SHIMON picks up a beer, takes a swig, then opens the door slightly. ABU DALO, *haggard, bearded, looks like he's crawled out of a sewer.*

SHIMON   What do you want?

ABU DALO   I've come for the room to rent, sir.

SHIMON   There's no room.

ABU DALO   *(looking around)* This is number six, isn't it?

SHIMON   I said there's no room for rent here.

ABU DALO   Do you live here?

SHIMON   Yes.

ABU DALO   Alone?

SHIMON   No.

ABU DALO   So you're married?

SHIMON   No.

ABU DALO   Well? Aren't you going to invite me in?

SHIMON   Of course not.

ABU DALO	I don't seem friendly?
SHIMON	You smell like shit.
ABU DALO	But I'm trying to be nice.
SHIMON	Niceness has nothing to do with how you smell.
ABU DALO	You're right. There's bad smell and there's bad people.
SHIMON	I like to distinguish between those who smell good and those who smell bad.
ABU DALO	That's a little peculiar.
SHIMON	I don't see it that way.
ABU DALO	What if I was a good person?
SHIMON	I don't care if you're a good person. You smell bad. Good day, shit pants. *(He slams the door shut.)*
ABU DALO	Don't care if I'm a good person? What the hell?
	I *like* the way I smell. In fact, I *choose* the way I smell. My smell is my humility. My humanity. I *own* my smell.
SHIMON	Who is this Arab asshole?
ABU DALO	You know you're not a man.
SHIMON	Fuck off.
ABU DALO	A man stops being a man when he no longer has any manners.

SHIMON *opens the door.*

SHIMON	Go away. Please. *(pulls out the Mauser)*

ABU DALO	Better. More respect in your tone. At least you sound genuine. Now we could really have a discussion.

ABU DALO pulls out a piece of paper. Hands it to SHIMON.

	Please. Read it.
SHIMON	No.
ABU DALO	We're going to get nowhere if you say no all the time.
SHIMON	I don't want to read it.
ABU DALO	You'll notice the official stamp in the bottom right-hand corner.
SHIMON	Screw the official stamp. Get off my property.
ABU DALO	Well that's just it. I'm entitled to this house.

SHIMON tears up the paper and eats it.

	Now how does this help us?
SHIMON	This is my house.
ABU DALO	No it's not.
SHIMON	You're a fucking Arab.
ABU DALO	Actually I have a name.
SHIMON	I'm not going to let a fucking Arab take my house—
ABU DALO	Abu Dalo's the name. And thirty-five years ago you took this house from me, Mr.—
SHIMON	This house was empty.
ABU DALO	We left our things in it.

SHIMON	Yeah, I heard some Arabs camped out some time ago.
ABU DALO	Camped out? For ten generations?
SHIMON	I was *given* this land.
ABU DALO	Good God you're difficult to talk to.
SHIMON	I'm difficult? You should try smelling yourself.

SHIMON points the gun at ABU DALO.

ABU DALO	Put that down already!
SHIMON	This gun is the hope of a nation.
ABU DALO	That's nice. I'm sure you and the gun are very good friends.
SHIMON	Best friends. *(SHIMON aims the gun.)* We've lived here for thirty-five years.
ABU DALO	We lived here for three hundred.
SHIMON	We returned after two thousand.

SHIMON points the gun at ABU DALO's head and cocks it.

ABU DALO pulls out a cigarette from behind his ear. Smokes.

	Don't smoke on my property.
ABU DALO	If I don't smoke, I get nervous. If I get nervous, I pee in my pants. Shit! I already have.
SHIMON	I don't believe this.
ABU DALO	Don't worry about it. It just adds to the overall smell of myself.
SHIMON	You just pissed yourself?
ABU DALO	Happens to the best of us.

SHIMON	You're revolting.
ABU DALO	That's my intention. To revolt. *(a beat)* 1967. I was sixteen years old. It was war and we lost. We were terrified. What were you going to do to us?
	There were soldiers. My family ran away to the village down the tracks. We were safe there. But we never gave up this house.
	For thirty-five years I wanted to see her again.
	I dreamt about her, imagined her, promised I'd come back.
	The house speaks to me.
THE HOUSE	Abu Dalo, is that you?
ABU DALO	*(laughing)* Habibi, how are you? I missed you so much.
THE HOUSE	What a nice... surprise.
ABU DALO	How is your cedar toilet seat? *(THE HOUSE laughs.)* And the fig tree my great-grandfather planted? God, I love that tree.

SHIMON puts down the gun.

Ya Habibi, I've come back.

Scene 5

ALEX upstairs, writing.

ALEX	Melissa raises her skirt and her legs shine her two fingers point beneath her white underwear.
	She has shaved so a man can better understand for to see is to understand.

MELISSA   "Clit-oris."

ALEX   She says.

Clit-oris? I say.
What's it do? I ask.

MELISSA   It *does* nothing. It *is* pleasure.

ALEX   You mean something exists only for the sake of pleasure?

MELISSA   Yup.

ALEX   *(writing)* This is what the Zionists should be fighting for.

So where is it? I say.

MELISSA   Look close.

ALEX   She says.

I can't see it, I say.

MELISSA   Look closer.

Radio sounds.

ALEX   Houston, this is Alex. We're ready to establish contact.

HOUSTON   Copy, Alex. What's your position?

ALEX   We've left the stratosphere and are approaching the clitoris.
But we're having trouble finding its precise location.

HOUSTON   Roger that, Alex. Keep a close eye on things and proceed with caution.
And remember what Wikipedia says: start slow, be sensitive and inventive.

ALEX   I look up, I look in.
It's really dark in here.
I can't see anything.

Hello? *(echo: hello, hello, hello)*
Echo! *(echo, echo, echo)*
Is anyone home? *(home, home, home)*

Enter MELISSA'S CLITORIS.

Who are you?

MELISSA'S CLITORIS
I'm Melissa's clitoris.

ALEX
Oh. At last! I found you.
Is the clitoris always located so deep in outer space?

MELISSA'S CLITORIS
It varies from woman to woman.

ALEX
How should I touch you?

MELISSA'S CLITORIS
Carefully.
I've got so much passion in me I'm like a bomb ready to go off.

ALEX
Do you know where I can find my mother?

Scene 6

THE CAMEL lights up a cigarette, addresses the audience.

THE CAMEL
I'm a camel. You've probably seen pictures of me. I've been in my share of movies too. Books, lots of books. Maybe you went on a tour, paid a lot of money to take a ride and watch the sun rise while you laughed at me shitting gumballs in the sand.

You're wondering. Why am I talking? What does a camel have to say to you?

Here in the Middle East a camel is a fly on the wall. Religions, loves, dreams, vows—all pass through the ears and eyes of the camel.

I know this entire country from top to bottom. I've met messed-up prophets, strange birds, crazy houses. I've known this house for some time now. There's something tragic and fucked up about her.

Kill or be killed. If you stay, that's what happens. Or you suffer from the fear. That's what it means to be a house in Jerusalem. To call this place home.

ABU DALO is outside THE HOUSE, drenched. SHIMON inside, drinking beer.

ALEX   Who's that out front?

SHIMON   Its name is Abu Dalo. And he's been standing there all night.

ALEX   In the rain?

SHIMON   He thinks this house is his. Don't open the door. Don't speak to him.

ALEX   I'm going to ask him a few questions.

SHIMON blocks the door.

SHIMON   Hold on, kid.
              We need to know what this moment means.
              Do we shoot the Arab or let him go in peace?
              Is he armed—and if so, with what?
              If we shoot him, there's blood on our hands—and the front step.
              If we let him go, he could come back to haunt us.
              Kill or be killed.
              Alex. I said no. *(ALEX opens the door.)*

ALEX   Good morning. Hey, you smell bad. You're a Palestinian.

ABU DALO   Do you want to shoot me too?

ALEX   No, sir. I just want to ask a few questions. Mr. Abu Dalo, are you married?

ABU DALO   Yes.

Enter RIVKA.

ALEX   Hi Rivka. *(to ABU DALO)* Have you ever given your wife cunnilingus before?

RIVKA enters THE HOUSE.

RIVKA   Who the hell is Alex talking to?

SHIMON   The enemy. *(SHIMON slams the door shut.)*

ALEX   I need you to tell me, sir, if you: a) practise cunnilingus, and b) if you consider yourself good at it.

ABU DALO Yes, I have given cunnilingus, infrequently, but I have never considered whether it was something I was good at. I simply did it.

ALEX   Interesting. And the subject's response?

ABU DALO Positive, I would say. *(ALEX writes down notes, etc.)*

SHIMON   What the hell is going on with my son? Why is he talking about oral sex to an Arab?

RIVKA   Well... that's what I wanted to talk to you about. I'm worried about Alex.

SHIMON   So am I.

ALEX   State your education.

ABU DALO Doctor of Literature.

ALEX   Occupation?

ABU DALO Former professor, Birzeit University. Writer of poetry, plays and articles.

ALEX   Really? I'm a writer too.

SHIMON	An educated Arab. You think he's telling the truth?
RIVKA	I have no idea. I've never met the guy. What's he doing here anyways?
SHIMON	Being a nuisance.
ALEX	Let me be frank. I need to recruit five hundred Palestinians into my legions, so please, answer the following questions honestly. When was the last time you engaged in the act of cunnilingus, Mr. Abu Dalo?
ABU DALO	1978.
ALEX	Wow. So you're like a museum piece. Fascinating. *(writing notes, etc.)*
RIVKA	You need to talk to your son.
SHIMON	I'll talk to him all right. Right after I figure out what to do with this stinking Arab. He's dangerous.
RIVKA	If he's a threat you should call the police.
SHIMON	The police can't help me with this. The house spoke to him.
RIVKA	Are you drunk?
SHIMON	This is a Jewish house. The house told me so—she spoke to me. But the house speaks to him too. So how does the Arab fit into this?

ALEX writing, taking notes with ABU DALO.

ALEX	Have you ever given cunnilingus to a Jewess?
ABU DALO	I told you I'm married.
ALEX	I'll take that as a "no." So where's your wife?
ABU DALO	Not here.

ALEX	Can I interview her sometime?
ABU DALO	NO.
ALEX	How often do you two copulate? Per annum.
ABU DALO	Shut up.
ALEX	Does she wear a head scarf?
ABU DALO	I don't want to talk about my wife.
ALEX	What does the Koran have to say about cunnilingus?
ABU DALO	Kid, I don't care what the hell the Koran says about anything. Now go into the backyard and spend some time with the fig tree. Try and learn from it. It knows the virtue of shutting the fuck up.
SHIMON	That's enough. I'm going outside.
RIVKA	Hold on. We need to talk.
ALEX	What fig tree?

ABU DALO leads ALEX into the backyard.

ABU DALO	The fig tree that my great-grandfather planted. Does this still lead to the backyard?

SHIMON and RIVKA go through the front door to look for them.

SHIMON	Alex? Where are you?
ABU DALO	Where the hell is it?
ALEX	I don't think we ever had a fig tree. Are you sure you lived here?
SHIMON	Alex? Come back inside!

ABU DALO   Of course I'm sure. It was right here. Ten feet tall. The most beautiful fig tree in the world! What kind of person would cut down a fig tree? *(a beat)* May I use your bathroom?

ALEX   I would be honoured, sir.

ALEX lets ABU DALO inside. ALEX searches for signs of the fig tree.

SHIMON   The boy never listens.

RIVKA   He's a teenager. You need to find new ways to talk. It's time, Shimon.

SHIMON   I've had enough talking.

RIVKA   The boy wants to know who his mother is.

SHIMON   He floated down the river in a basket. And that's all there is to say.

RIVKA   Tell him the truth.

SHIMON   My son is a miracle.
His life is a miracle.
But the world corrupts him.
That's why he doesn't listen.
People like you make him lost.

RIVKA   I've been like a mother to your son. I'm his teacher.

SHIMON   My book will be his teacher. He will learn the story of the gun.
The miracle of this country.

RIVKA   Enough with the fairy tales. He's growing up.

SHIMON   Leave us, Rivka—it's time to move on.
Get married. Meet someone your own age.
Have your own kids.

RIVKA   You're getting rid of me.

RIVKA exits. SHIMON opens a beer.

ALEX	Hey, was there ever a fig tree out back?
SHIMON	Alex! Are you okay?
ALEX	I'm fine. The Arab's nice—and he's a writer.
SHIMON	Where the hell is he?
ALEX	*(ignores him)* He's going to join me in my revolutionary peace efforts. Though his practices are somewhat out of date.

ABU DALO pulls a radio out from his coat. He turns it on. Arabic pop music.

SHIMON	What the hell is that?
ALEX	It's Abu Dalo.
SHIMON	You let him inside?
ALEX	Yeah.
SHIMON	Are you totally out of your mind?
ALEX	He had to urinate.
SHIMON	*(knocks on the door)* Abu Dalo! Get out of my bathroom! Abu Dalo!
	My God. This is a disaster. Do you understand what this means?
ALEX	It means there's a stranger in our restroom.
SHIMON	This changes everything. He's in the house. How could you do this?
ALEX	I didn't do anything.
SHIMON	You let the enemy in. Abu Dalo! Abu Dalo, open this door!

Enter THE CAMEL and THE HOUSE.

THE CAMEL	You're looking really good today, sweetheart. Especially from the back.
THE HOUSE	I hate it when you objectify me. Especially since you've been gone for six months. How was Sinai?
THE CAMEL	Not as beautiful as you.
THE HOUSE	There are cobwebs in the corners of the living room. There's mould between the floorboards. Peeling paint, broken pipes, an eroding foundation. I'm worried I'm going to get condemned—they'll tear me down and put a road right through to that new mall they're building.
THE CAMEL	Humans. Messy species.
THE HOUSE	Shimon used to be good to me. But every year he gets worse. He ignores the details. I'm the kind of house who believes that someone better will come along and finally take care of me.
THE CAMEL	I could take care of you.
THE HOUSE	You told me you're "allergic to the domestic."
THE CAMEL	That was a crass and thoughtless comment. I've changed.
THE HOUSE	A domestic camel? I'll believe it when I see it.
THE CAMEL	And that Arab's domestic? When was the last time he took a shower?
THE HOUSE	He's an old friend.
THE CAMEL	He's weaving and muttering to the sink and the bathtub.
THE HOUSE	He cares about me. He's very passionate.

The Arabic music blasts at high volume ("Habibi, Habibi": a love song to THE HOUSE). ABU DALO does some crazy dance and lip-synchs.

THE CAMEL	He seems a bit fucked up, if you ask me.

THE HOUSE	He knows what I need.
ABU DALO	One is away for so many years. One lives in another house. Many houses.
	(to THE HOUSE) For all those years, when I was in exile, when I was in jail, you were all I could think of. I dreamt of your floorboards. I memorized every detail, and whatever I couldn't remember I made up.
	It's so good to be here. Are you happy to see me too? *(a beat)*
	I know, you probably thought I was dead. That I'd never come back.
	But you know I can treat you so much better than that Jewish prick.
	I missed you, very, very much.
THE HOUSE	You're sitting on the throne.
ABU DALO	Real cedar. A joy on the rumpus.
THE HOUSE	The toilet gets a bad rap. Nobody really wants to talk about toilets. People say, "nice bathroom."
ABU DALO	Nice bathroom.
THE HOUSE	Or, "lovely bath."
ABU DALO	Lovely bath.
THE HOUSE	Or, "I like the mirror you've put in."
ABU DALO	It is a nice addition.
THE HOUSE	But how many people can say, "I love your toilet"?
ABU DALO	I *love* your toilet. You know, I've always thought the toilet is the heart of the house. It's not unlike an altar.

You bring your offerings. And they're left in the earth.

ABU DALO flushes the toilet. He stands up.

THE HOUSE   Well, well, Abu Dalo. It's time. Wash up.

ABU DALO   I'm afraid I can't do that.

THE HOUSE   To commemorate your return you need to clean up.

ABU DALO   My filth is my penance.

THE HOUSE   Then you've served your time, Abu Dalo.

ABU DALO   No I haven't.

THE HOUSE   What could you have done to make yourself smell this bad?

ABU DALO   I can't say.

THE HOUSE   You're ashamed.

ABU DALO   I don't want to talk about it.

THE HOUSE   But your smell insults me.

ABU DALO   I choose to smell this way. To make myself ugly.

THE HOUSE   Are you married?

ABU DALO   Yes.

THE HOUSE   What's her name?

ABU DALO   Yuad.

THE HOUSE   I love that name: Yuad. It rolls off the tongue like water off an eaves-trough. When is she coming?

ABU DALO   It's complicated. We haven't actually talked in three years.

THE HOUSE	Well what are you waiting for? Call her.

ABU DALO	What if Yuad doesn't want to hear from me? I can barely remember what she looks like.

THE HOUSE	Does she know about me?

ABU DALO	Of course she does. I used to talk to her about you all the time.

THE HOUSE	Then tell Yuad you're bringing her home. You'll be a normal husband and wife again. You'll have a child.

ABU DALO	We already have one.

THE HOUSE	Abu Dalo, why didn't you just say so!

ABU DALO	Because... I don't know. I haven't seen her since she was a baby. She's fifteen.

THE HOUSE	When you were sixteen, and you were preparing to leave, you made me a promise: you said you'd come back and take care of me. And I said, don't come back until you have a wife and child. Until you're ready. You're ready, Abu Dalo. Fulfill your promise.

ABU DALO	A promise is one thing. But putting it into practice is something else. I don't even know how to talk to them.

THE HOUSE	You'll do just fine. Call your wife. I promise: if you want me, you will get me. And you need to look good for when your family comes. Lather up. Use good, hot water. Make yourself new.

Enter SHIMON.

SHIMON	Abu Dalo?

He tries the door. It's locked. He tries the door again.

Open up, you moron. I promise... I won't kill you.

Silence.

I want to kill you, but I won't. We can negotiate. You give me something, I give you something. We'll figure it out. We're men! We're civilized!

A beat.

Abu Dalo? Let's talk.

Knocks.

You little Arab turd. Open up! This is MY BATHROOM! This is MY HOUSE!

ABU DALO opens up the cabinet. Pulls out a bar of soap. A razor. He turns on the water and starts to clean his face.

THE CAMEL   It's like watching a train wreck.

THE HOUSE   I haven't felt this hopeful since Oslo.

THE CAMEL   This has disaster written all over it. You've promised yourself to both of them.

THE HOUSE   I'm looking for life. And here it is, right between these walls.

THE CAMEL   They'll fuck you up. Guaranteed.

THE HOUSE   The difference between you and me is I believe in people.

THE CAMEL   The difference between you and me is you're completely unrealistic.

THE HOUSE   People exhibit unusual and unexpected potentials. That is their beauty.

ALEX in SHIMON's room. He snoops around, knocking on the floor, searching for a hollow place.

THE CAMEL   So why's the kid snooping around his father's room?

THE HOUSE   Oh dear.

ALEX tries to pry open a floorboard.

THE CAMEL	With a crowbar? He doesn't need to be so rough with you.

ALEX removes the floorboard. Searching inside he finds an ammunitions box.

	What's in the ammo box?
THE HOUSE	More gentlemen's magazines, I suppose.
THE CAMEL	Nobody hides smut under nailed-down floorboards.
	I don't have a good feeling about this.
THE HOUSE	All knowledge is good, right?
THE CAMEL	You know what they say about knowledge. It's like a renovation. It changes you.

Scene 7

Eight days pass. SHIMON and ABU DALO at the table. ABU DALO is clean-shaven and wearing SHIMON's clothes.

SHIMON	Now. My son is drawing up a contract for us based on last night's final round of talks.
ABU DALO	"For eight days and eight nights, the Palestinian defied the oppression of his enemy and barricaded himself in a toilet." How's that for an opening?
SHIMON	You could've ended the occupation of my toilet earlier.
ABU DALO	You would've shot me.
SHIMON	I would've fed you.
ABU DALO	I don't need your food.
SHIMON	No. Of course not. You ate all of my toothpaste and Aspirin instead.

ABU DALO	"And when the Palestinian opened the bathroom cabinet, he saw there were only enough Tums for one day. But lo and behold, a great miracle occurred. And the Tums lasted for eight days and eight nights."
SHIMON	Shut up.
ABU DALO	I really like Tums. They're nice on the stomach.
SHIMON	I should never have negotiated with you.
ABU DALO	I would've stayed in there longer had you kept the fig tree in the back. If you hadn't cut down that fig tree, I could've eaten figs till the cows came home.
SHIMON	I cut down that tree years ago.
ABU DALO	My great-grandfather planted that tree.
SHIMON	And then some bugs came and ate it. What do you want me to say? I'm sorry your friggin' fig tree died.
ABU DALO	You have no respect.
SHIMON	While I had to shit and piss in my own backyard, I brought you food. Dates. Almonds. Pistachios. Blood oranges—
ABU DALO	I detest pity.
SHIMON	That wasn't pity. That was me not wanting a dead Arab stinking up my bathroom. So. Are we doing this or not?
ABU DALO	*I* write *your* story.
SHIMON	You're a writer. You write my story.
ABU DALO	I *was* a writer.
SHIMON	Professor of Arabic literature.
ABU DALO	That's the past.

SHIMON	I tell you what to say. You make it sound flowery and good.
ABU DALO	Sure. And you're really going to give me half this house?
SHIMON	For as long we work on this book.
ABU DALO	All right. Which half?
SHIMON	I don't know. We didn't work out the specifics.
ABU DALO	Well maybe we should.
SHIMON	O-kay.
ABU DALO	I want my old room.
SHIMON	Fine.
ABU DALO	I want the toilet.
SHIMON	We share the toilet.
ABU DALO	It spoke to me.
SHIMON	The whole house spoke to me. 1967. The landscape was full of stealing and lies. The bodies roasting in the sun. And this house appeared before me like a miracle. She promised herself to me. This is a Jewish house.
ABU DALO	Your vision was a lie. The house speaks to me. You heard her.
SHIMON	It doesn't mean she's your house.
ABU DALO	Yes it does.
SHIMON	No, it means... we have to negotiate.
ABU DALO	I want this room.
SHIMON	I work in here.

ABU DALO	Where will I work?
SHIMON	In here with me.
ABU DALO	This arrangement is unacceptable.
SHIMON	You occupying my bathroom for eight days is unacceptable. I could have had you arrested. I still could. Would you like that?
ABU DALO	Fuck you.
SHIMON	Would you like to be deported?

Silence.

	Would you like me to shoot you?
ABU DALO	That would be murder.
SHIMON	Not if I tell the police that some filthy Arab forced his way into my house. *(picking up the gun, pointing it)* You have to help me write this book. And we better live in fucking peace, you pain in the ass.
ABU DALO	I want a DustBuster.
SHIMON	I have a vacuum cleaner. You can borrow that.
ABU DALO	I won't agree to anything unless you buy me a DustBuster.
SHIMON	What the hell do you need a DustBuster for?
ABU DALO	They're efficient, practical and they get into small places.
SHIMON	My vacuum cleaner has changeable heads.
ABU DALO	I'm not writing a word without the DustBuster.
SHIMON	Oh God.

ABU DALO	This place is a pigsty. The DustBuster is the essence of cleanliness. I even know the model I want. There's a blond woman on the package in a tight red dress bent over, happily DustBusting. I promise to be as happy as that woman if you buy me that DustBuster.
SHIMON	All right. I'll buy it, I'll buy it. Just shut up already. We need to get started.
ABU DALO	Why are you negotiating with me? Why not just have me arrested?
SHIMON	I'm writing this book for my son.
ABU DALO	So why don't you just write this book yourself?
SHIMON	I'm about to give you half this house and you're asking why?

SHIMON pulls out the Mauser.

ABU DALO	Not this again.
SHIMON	I want you to call her "Golda." She's going to help us write. Aren't you, Golda?

He puts it menacingly onto the table.

ABU DALO	Well. Now that we've settled things I feel a whole lot better. Shall we?
SHIMON	Title: *The General and His Son: The Story of a Nation.* How is that?
ABU DALO	Arrogant as hell.
SHIMON	Perfect. *(ABU DALO types.)*
	"The General was born the child of German... something or others."
ABU DALO	Intellectuals?
SHIMON	Whatever. "His father, a psychotherapist. His mother, a lousy poet. His parents lived in Berlin where they held saloons every Thursday afternoon—"

ABU DALO	Salons—
SHIMON	"—entertaining the crème of the crème of European art. Writers from Moscow. Maya..." something or other.
ABU DALO	Mayakovsky.
SHIMON	Fuck it, I can't remember the other names. Make something up.
ABU DALO	Proust. I like Proust.
SHIMON	Whoever. "There were painters from Paris. Academics from London. Some guy named Bertolt Brecht came by and created a drink called the Rottweiler. Coffee, American bourbon and a dash of gasoline." I make none of this up. "For years, his parents were the centre of artistic and intellectual bullshit."
ABU DALO	Bullshit?
SHIMON	"It was his parents' intelligence, after all, that led them to their fates. In 1943, the General's parents were tragically escorted to the gas chambers."
ABU DALO	Uh huh.
SHIMON	"While the General, at the age of two, was hidden beneath a convent. And by war's end he saw everything as... Well. Dark." How do you like that?
ABU DALO	You should consider publishing this. The Holocaust sells.
SHIMON	Of course it sells. It's an original story. It's not every day six million people are systematically slaughtered. "The General couldn't speak until age six.

He ended up in a displaced persons camp in southern Germany. It was there he had to choose his fate: learn how to read or how to fix an engine. He chose the engine. Survival. His legacy. What he gave to a son."

ABU DALO   You can't read? *(a beat)* And so you can't write then? *(a beat)* Well. Things are becoming a little clearer now.

SHIMON   You'll be my eyes.

ABU DALO   How the hell do you live without being able to read?

SHIMON   I live with my hands.

ABU DALO   But street signs and can labels. The basics.

SHIMON   I manage just fine.

ABU DALO   Who's ever heard of a general who can't read or write?

SHIMON   I got by just fine.

ABU DALO   Why didn't you ever learn?

SHIMON   I just said. The engine or the book. It was one or the other.

ABU DALO   People have been known to do both.

SHIMON   Not me. I was *chosen* not to read or write. That was my fate. Words slip off my eyes like water off a stone.

ABU DALO   Who are you? Really.

SHIMON   Aren't we going to find that out?

ABU DALO   Is this book going to be about the truth?

SHIMON   Yes.

ABU DALO   Then you have to tell me the truth.

SHIMON	All right.
ABU DALO	*(typing)* "The General had a natural inclination toward fixing things, and thus made those around him stronger."
SHIMON	Yes.
ABU DALO	"While the Holocaust rendered him an atheist, the General became a believer thanks to the vision he had of the house."
SHIMON	True.
ABU DALO	"A twist of fate brought us his co-biographer: the Palestinian."
SHIMON	Good.
ABU DALO	"Illiterate and compassionate, the General has a deep-seated need to understand the enemy. To fix all problems. To maintain the engine of his country."
SHIMON	"It was in that spirit the Palestinian and Jew forged a bond. Brought together by circumstance, fate, destiny."

SHIMON picks up the gun and starts to polish it.

ABU DALO	"This is a story, told from one man to his enemy. And from his enemy to the world."
SHIMON	Introduction.

Scene 8

The same day. ALEX's bedroom. Reading.

ALEX	"As my father's generation was so focused on fighting for this land, on war as the only solution to dealing with our enemies, of pushing forward, hard against them, into land, we, as followers of the *Cunnilingus Manifesto*, hereby renounce the act of copulation in favour of ten years strict cunnilingual training. It is possible that at the end of this process we may return to an era that would involve penetration.

This thesis—antithesis line of progression is otherwise known as cunnilingual materialism."

RIVKA   Alex, we need to be quiet. Your dad can't know I'm here.

ALEX   What was my dad like when he was younger?

RIVKA   He was fearless. Had so much energy he couldn't sit still. But he always said you were the best thing that happened to him. You calmed him right down.

ALEX   So he was a good general?

RIVKA   One of the best.

ALEX   Was he a good man?

RIVKA   Of course. He took care of you. He raised you by himself.

ALEX   You ever live with someone for years, but realize at a certain point that you don't actually know who they are?

RIVKA   Sure. That's what being in a family's all about.

ALEX   I don't know my father at all. He talks about the army all the time, his achievements and successes, yet he has no medals. He remembers entire vistas where battles were fought, down to the exact stone, and yet there are no pictures. He talks about the buddies he fought with, but none of them ever drop by. None of it adds up.

RIVKA   Your father's a strange man. I mean, he's a survivor, you know?

ALEX   Why did he leave the army at such an early age?

RIVKA   To take care of you, of course.

ALEX   Right. (writing)

RIVKA   What are you writing?

ALEX	None of your business.
RIVKA	What's wrong?
ALEX	What's wrong is that everything is becoming so much more clear. You. My father. You're in on this together. Hiding things from me.
RIVKA	I hide nothing from you.
ALEX	Of course you do.
RIVKA	What are you writing?
ALEX	It's not important.
RIVKA	Read it to me.
ALEX	*(a beat)* Okay. On one condition: you say yes.
RIVKA	Yes what?
ALEX	Yes, I'll let Alex practise his cunnilingus—
RIVKA	Are you trying to blackmail me into having sex with you?
ALEX	I don't want sex, Rivka. I want to give you cunnilingus.
RIVKA	*(a beat)* They're sending me to Hebron next week. I'll be working the checkpoint.
ALEX	Well, have fun protecting whacked-out settlers and shooting at little kids who throw stones.
RIVKA	I believe in this. It's my duty. It's my choice. Tell me what you wrote, Alex.
ALEX	Chapter Three:
	"No legionnaires of the *Cunnilingus Manifesto* may join the armed forces of any nation, nor will they bear arms, condoms or parachutes."

RIVKA   You have to do your service.

ALEX   I can refuse. I'll just say I'm not Israeli.

RIVKA   Don't be an idiot. Of course you're Israeli.

ALEX   I floated down the river in a basket. Come here. I want to practise my
             cunnilingual materialism.

RIVKA   Alex. What the fuck's gotten into you?

ALEX   I'm trying to get deeper into this. You know. Trying to figure out what
             this manifesto is really about.

RIVKA   It's about being fifteen. Whatever. *(a beat)* Why don't you just hold
             me?

ALEX   Hold you?

RIVKA   We can lie on your bed. And you can hold me.

ALEX   Why on earth would I do that?

RIVKA   *(a beat)* Did you hear that Ilan Ramon—

ALEX   Not interested. It's the wrong science, Rivka. I don't care about outer
             space anymore.

RIVKA   But you love him. He went up in the shuttle today.

ALEX   Ilan Ramon was so fourteen.
             Fifteen is the dawn of a whole new age.
             Goodbye Rivka.

             Exit RIVKA. ALEX opens up the ammunitions box and starts to read from its contents.

THE CAMEL   Today the astronaut Ilan Ramon boarded the space shuttle *Columbia*
             and left everything behind:
             Fig trees, toilets, manifestos, checkpoints—
             this messy world full of messy humans.

Truth is, sometimes you gotta get away—
perspective is important when it comes to situations as complex as
the Middle East.
Who is right and who is wrong? Who does this house belong to?
What are we to make of the history of these men?
Ilan Ramon has to go so far to get perspective he's gone all the way
to outer space.

There he is—I can see him. He is the hope of a nation.
He's a light unto nations.
He's up there, listening to a universe without promises.
Maybe he can even hear the sound of peace.

Scene 9

A few days later. ABU DALO sitting at the typewriter. SHIMON drinking beer.

ABU DALO   "And the land speaks in the language of our forefathers."

SHIMON   Read that passage over to me again.

ABU DALO   "1988. The Jordan–Israel border.

The day was like any other in the West Bank. Past the Palestinian
farmers and their olive trees, the Jewish settlers and their melodic
prayers. Here you can see the rocky hillsides, the rushing waters of
the Jordan River. Here the air is clear, the sun is gold, and the land
speaks in the language of our forefathers."

SHIMON   Oh yes. I like that.

ABU DALO typing.

ABU DALO   "Dusk was coming in like a sail. The General took heart in the darkness, in the shadows thick like leaves—"

SHIMON   Okay, okay, enough poetry—

Enter ALEX.

ABU DALO	"When, all of a sudden, a basket came drifting by—"
SHIMON	That's right, a basket—no bigger than my leg—
ABU DALO	"No bigger than our hero's thigh—"
SHIMON	What the fuck, I said.
ABU DALO	"'What is it before my eyes?' He asked the heavens."
SHIMON	A baby.
ABU DALO	"A child."
SHIMON	Alone on the river.
ABU DALO	"Floating on the tears of his mother."
SHIMON	Oh. I like that.
ABU DALO	"Who this boy's mother was, what he was doing in the basket, is a mystery, one that haunts both hero and son."
SHIMON	No. There was no torment. No haunting.
ABU DALO	Then it was a vision.
SHIMON	I picked up the baby—
ABU DALO	(typing) "While the First Intifada simmered in the universities of Ramallah and in the streets of Nablus, a miracle occurred."
SHIMON	Yes!
ABU DALO	(typing) "The General brought life into his arms—"
SHIMON	I brought him home. I gave him a bris and raised him myself. "Thus the General's second vision made manifest the first: a child. To fulfill his promise to the house, at last."

ALEX	Question. What were you doing by the Jordan River?
SHIMON	I was washing my hands.
ALEX	Why were they dirty?
SHIMON	Work. It was hot. The air was full of dust and sweat.
ALEX	What sort of work?
SHIMON	I was Brigadier General of the West Bank Division. Central Command.
ALEX	What does such a general do?
SHIMON	He protects the land.
ALEX	Can you be more specific?

ABU DALO typing.

SHIMON	"The General protected Judea and Samaria, the land given to his people, as the old prophets prophesied. And he engaged with his enemies. Fearlessly."
ALEX	What about the normal people living in the West Bank? Were they the enemy too?
SHIMON	Some were. It's difficult to separate good from bad, foe from friend.
ALEX	Were mistakes made?
SHIMON	Of course mistakes were made. It's the nature of war.
ALEX	How did you feel when you saw people living in refugee camps and not homes?
SHIMON	A general cannot make decisions based on a feeling. A general must try to uphold the moral standard, objectively and precisely. He must do his job. End of chapter.

Exit SHIMON.

ALEX   It's a bit strange a former Israeli general has a Palestinian writing for him.

ABU DALO   Your father's a strange man. He says he can't read or write.

ALEX   Do you have any books published, Mr. Abu Dalo?

ABU DALO   A few. I wrote them many years ago. And they're not in your libraries.

ALEX   So the books got you in trouble.

ABU DALO   You could say that.

ALEX   Hmmm. I admire that. Getting in trouble for writing something you believe in is, like, every writer's dream.

ABU DALO   I suppose. If you consider prison romantic.

ALEX   My father's book is totally boring.

ABU DALO   It's full of lies.

ALEX   So why are you helping him write it? *(a beat)* Are you a liar too?

ABU DALO   *(sarcastically)* No. Everything I say and do is one hundred percent honest.

ALEX   I never lie.

ABU DALO   Then you're one in a million, kid.

            Look, let me give you some advice: when and if you ever grow up, you'll learn that everyone lies. It's what being an adult is all about: pretending you're something that you're not. The successful ones are those who pull it off.

ALEX   Yeah, well I guess my father is a pretty rotten failure then.

ALEX shows ABU DALO the ammunitions box. Opens it up to reveal its contents. ABU DALO reads the documents inside.

ABU DALO   Where'd you get this?

ALEX   I found it.

ABU DALO reads some more.

ABU DALO   Do you realize what you have here?

ALEX   I think so.

ABU DALO   Does he know you found this?

ALEX   He doesn't have a clue.

ABU DALO   Why are you showing this to me?

ALEX   Mr. Abu Dalo, you can have this on one condition: you do something with it.

ABU DALO   I'm going to do the only thing I can: take it to the press. I'll humiliate him. That's what you want, isn't it?

Exit ALEX.

THE HOUSE enters.

It's the only choice I have. Publish or perish. You should be all mine. You have to be all mine. It's the only weapon I have. It's the only thing I can do to him. I talked to my daughter Suha. She said they'd be here today.

I didn't even recognize her voice. I thought it was Yuad I was talking to. She's fifteen now.

THE HOUSE   Tell me your first morning.

ABU DALO   Yuad is in bed, sleeping. I get up early and sweep your floors. I make some coffee, then I clean the bathroom—

THE HOUSE   I like a clean bathroom.

ABU DALO   I wake up my daughter with a kiss on the forehead. We go to the corner store—I buy her cardamom cookies, and I buy myself a newspaper. I come home and read it—right here—cover to cover. She sits across from me, eating her cookies. And I don't worry that someone's going to knock on the door and arrest me. I don't worry about bombs, bulldozers or police. Because you protect me. I don't worry at all anymore. I'm a new person.

THE HOUSE   A renovation.

ABU DALO   What should I wear?

THE HOUSE   Something clean.

ABU DALO   I was thinking of buying Yuad a bed.

THE HOUSE   A bed is like the sail of a ship.

ABU DALO   We'll have great dinners. We'll sit on the bed together and read to each other.

THE HOUSE   This will be an Arab house. This will be your home.

ABU DALO   We'll be a normal family.

Enter SUHA *singing "Should I Stay or Should I Go." She knocks on the door.* ABU DALO *opens it. Enter* SUHA *carrying a Ziploc bag with fleshy red bits in one hand and a pigeon in a cage in the other.*

SUHA AS GROUCHO
            Home delivery for Mr. Abu Dalo.

ABU DALO   What is it?

SUHA AS GROUCHO
            Your wife.

ABU DALO   Excuse me?

SUHA   She was watching *The Simpsons* and there was an accident.

She loved *The Simpsons*. It was the only thing that made her laugh.

Eight o'clock, every day, the TV'd come on. By 8:03, you'd be guaranteed she'd laugh. Like clockwork.

ABU DALO   What are you talking about?

SUHA AS GROUCHO
            Your wife.

ABU DALO   My wife is going to be here this afternoon.

SUHA AS GROUCHO
            This is your wife.

SUHA   You should be grateful. It's a miracle I was able to hold on to this much of her.

SUHA AS GROUCHO
            Do you know how difficult it was just to find her fingers?

SUHA   Well, I didn't find the fingers. The police did. At least they're good for something.

ABU DALO   *(a beat)* Suha? Is that you?

SUHA   Tell us a joke, Groucho.

SUHA AS GROUCHO
            What do fathers and squares have in common? *(a beat)*

            They're never around.

ABU DALO   I see you've grown up into a mature young woman.
            It's good to see you.
            Where's your mother?

   SUHA points to the Ziploc bag.

            Don't make those kinds of jokes. It's disgusting.

| SUHA | This isn't a joke. |

| ABU DALO | Are you here to laugh at me? |

| SUHA | I can't laugh.
If I laugh, I might faint.
If I faint, I could go into a coma. |

SUHA AS GROUCHO

The goyl has cataplexy. A rare neuy-ral dis-oyder.
She can't experience extreme emotions without falling down.
Ha, ha, ha, ha, ha.

| ABU DALO | You're crazy. I'm going inside to make some coffee. You can come in when your mother is here. |

| SUHA | Your Yuad died.
Three years ago.
In the middle of *The Simpsons*
a rain of mortar fell on our house.
She was laughing.
I ran home from the store.
I swear the entire courtyard turned purple with her blood.
Purple stone,
purple columns,
purple flowers.
Your Yuad always wanted to be a painter.
But it was only when she died that she got the colours right. |

You know what pisses me off? The whole situation could've been avoided. If you'd have been there like you should've, none of this would've happened.

SUHA tries to hand ABU DALO the Ziploc bag.

SUHA AS GROUCHO

At least she doesn't smell bad. I kept her in the freezer. I had to label the Ziploc with her name.

| ABU DALO | Uch! Get this away from me. |

SUHA	Don't you want it?
ABU DALO	No!
SUHA	You need to bury her.
ABU DALO	There's nothing to bury.
SUHA	Yes there is.
ABU DALO	I can't bury a Ziploc.
SUHA	Yes you can. She wanted to come home. It was her final wish, Father—
ABU DALO	Don't call me that—
SUHA	DON'T BE SUCH A WIMP! *(calmly)* You have to bury her. It's your responsibility.
ABU DALO	Why didn't anyone tell me?
SUHA	You stopped calling. For three years. We never heard from you.

SUHA AS GROUCHO
    We never hoyd from you.

ABU DALO	Would you stop it with that?
SUHA	Meet my pigeon. Groucho.
ABU DALO	Groucho?

SUHA AS GROUCHO
    I'm a rare comedic boyd. My jokes are so bad I make sure she won't laugh.

SUHA	Tell us a joke, Groucho.

SUHA AS GROUCHO
    What do you call a man with a bag?

SUHA throws the bag to ABU DALO. He drops it.

A doyt bag.

SUHA   Bad joke. Bad joke, Jew.

ABU DALO   He's a pigeon.

SUHA   He's a Jewish pigeon. Look at his nose.

ABU DALO   It's called a beak.

SUHA   It's a Jewish nose. *(She spits on the bird.)*

ABU DALO   You're really screwed up.

ABU DALO leaves. SUHA opens the cage. Groucho won't fly.

SUHA   Fly, Groucho.
                (whistling, etc.) Fly, Groucho.
                Fly, asshole of a Jew!
                There you have it. Doesn't even want to leave his cage.

SUHA AS GROUCHO
                Fucking fathers. Fucking fucks. Fuck. Fuck. Fuck.

Enter ALEX. He peers outside the door.

ALEX   Houston, this is Alex. We've identified a female Arab in the house.
                We're ready to establish contact.

HOUSTON   Copy that. You be careful in there.

SUHA   Shut up and get me a shovel.

ALEX   Is this what you always say to men you first meet?

SUHA stares him up and down, as though noticing him for the first time.

SUHA   You're not a man.

ALEX   Yes I am. I'll prove it to you.

SUHA	Shut up, kike, and get me a shovel.
ALEX	I don't have a shovel.
SUHA	What kind of a man doesn't have a shovel?
ALEX	The kind of man that doesn't want to be your typical kind of man.
SUHA	What's your typical kind of man?
ALEX	The kind that has a shovel.
SUHA	Jew, you're annoying.
ALEX	No, I'm just diligent with my language.
SUHA	I don't know you yet. But I sense that I might come to truly hate you.
ALEX	Now *you* talk like a man.
SUHA	That's funny. Because I don't even want to talk. I just want a shovel.
ALEX	How very distant and man-like.
SUHA	Piss off.
ALEX	Judging by your behaviour, I'm willing to bet you've never had cunnilingus.
SUHA	I'll bet you're right.
ALEX	I'll bet you don't even know what it is.
SUHA	Does it involve extreme sensation?
ALEX	Guaranteed.
SUHA	I want none of it.
ALEX	I'm perfectly serious when I say I've been waiting for a subject like you my whole life. You're the Palestinian of my dreams.

SUHA	Screw off.

ALEX	You're the hope of peace between nations.

SUHA	Good God.

ALEX	I had a vision of you. And you came. Together we can save the Middle East!

SUHA	Leave me THE FUCK ALONE!

SUHA faints.

ALEX	Hello? Hello? Are you okay? Hello?

ALEX climbs on top of her and starts to give her mouth-to-mouth.

SUHA	Do I know you?

ALEX	We just met.

SUHA	What were you just doing?

ALEX	Giving you mouth-to-mouth.

SUHA	What was I doing?

ALEX	Looking for a shovel.

SUHA	Why?

ALEX	I don't know. We didn't get that far yet.

SUHA	How far did we get?

ALEX	We managed to have our first fight. You said I wasn't a man. So I said you were a man. You tried to ignore me. I pestered, you yelled, then fainted. I resuscitated.

SUHA	*(wiping her mouth)* You were kissing me.

ALEX	It's called mouth-to-mouth resuscitation.
SUHA	Well there you have it. I let you get under my skin.
ALEX	Damn it. I didn't even know I was under it. I'm very good at annoying people.
SUHA	I have cataplexy, okay? A rare neural disorder. I can't experience extreme emotions.
ALEX	Oh. So I guess this means I can't give you cunnilingus.
SUHA	What's that?
ALEX	The sexual stimulation of a woman's genitals employing tongue and lips.
SUHA	I guess not.
	Where do you come from?
ALEX	There's a high likelihood I'm the test-tube baby of the Dalai Lama and Woody Allen.
SUHA	The Dalai Lama would never donate his sperm to a lab.
ALEX	You never know.

SUHA AS GROUCHO
Can you imagine the Dalai Lama whacking off into a jar?

They both start to laugh. SUHA *catches herself.*

SUHA	Damn it. Tell me something boring. Tell me about yourself.
ALEX	I'm a writer and I'm writing a book and I used to love Ilan Ramon but I don't anymore did you know that he used to fly F16s in the '80s and once he even flew into Iraq I wonder if the Iraqi shovel is the same as the Israeli shovel you should see the shovels my father has iron shovels plastic shovels pickaxe shovels we even have spoons which is really a kind of shovel—I can get you one—

SUHA	I remember now. I wanted the shovel so my father and I could bury my mother. She wanted to be buried here.
ALEX	*(a beat)* Oh.
SUHA	Get me a shovel.
ALEX	I never had a mother.
SUHA	Everyone has a mother.
ALEX	My father says I didn't.
SUHA	My father's a lying, cowardly cur who knows shit about shit.
ALEX	My father's a liar too.
	Do you drink orange Tang?
SUHA	Sometimes. Why?
ALEX	I just wanted to know. How different you are than me. I mean, I like orange Tang. A lot.
SUHA	It does leave a stupid mark on the lips.
ALEX	I could get you some if you want.
SUHA	I suppose I'd like that.
ALEX	Where are you from?
SUHA	Jenin.
ALEX	Do they have normal things in Jenin?
SUHA	We have orange Tang.

ALEX brings out two glasses of orange Tang. They drink them at the same time.

ALEX	Your pigeon's dead.
SUHA	I know.
ALEX	Is that why you like it?
SUHA	Don't ask me stupid questions.
ALEX	Do you have any friends?
SUHA	Not really.
ALEX	Me neither. My father did something so awful it makes me sick to know the truth.
SUHA	Yeah, well the truth is liable to make anyone puke their guts out.
ALEX	For some reason I like talking to you.
SUHA	Get me a shovel.
ALEX	Do you want me to help you bury your mother?

SUHA faints. Blackout.

End of Act I.

Act II

Scene 1

ABU DALO is drunk and alone, playing Scratch 'n Win. Each time he takes a card he scratches it, loses, then throws it into a huge pile. Every time he throws the card he makes a "woo" sound as it glides through the air.

ABU DALO Eight hundred and seven. Eight hundred and eight. Eight hundred and nine.

Enter SHIMON with a beer in hand.

SHIMON What the hell is going on here?

ABU DALO Eight hundred and ten.

SHIMON What is this shit all over the floor?

ABU DALO Eight hundred and eleven.

SHIMON What are you doing?

ABU DALO Scratch. And lose. Heh, heh, heh. Eight hundred and twelve.

SHIMON smells him for booze.

SHIMON   Are you drunk?

ABU DALO   Absolutely not. I'm a Muslim. Muslims don't drink. We're the most boring, stiff-faced losers on this planet. We fly airplanes into skyscrapers for fun. We can't look at a cartoon without killing people. Where's our sense of humour? I want a sense of humour! Make me laugh, Jew. And make me win. Eight hundred and thirteen. Eight hundred and fourteen...

SHIMON   I'm making you some coffee, you drunk Arab pig. Sober up. We need to get to work.

ABU DALO   I am working.

SHIMON   Yes, you're working at annoying me.

ABU DALO   Science! Much more practical than literature. I bought one thousand Scratch 'n Wins. Hypothesis: A man can go on such a nasty losing streak that he loses everything: House. Family. Soul. Become a black hole of loss. Woo!

SHIMON   You need to think a little more positive, Abu Dalo. Here. Drink this.

SHIMON brings him coffee. ABU DALO starts to drink. Spits it out.

ABU DALO   The least you Jews could do is learn how to make good coffee. You stole our falafel. Why don't you steal our coffee too?

ALEX and SUHA in the basement.

ALEX   And so I was floating in a basket on the Jordan River—

SUHA   Got the flashlights?

ALEX   Roger that. And my father found me. Pretty amazing, huh?

SUHA   Uch. It stinks down here.

ALEX	It's a root cellar. What were you expecting?
SHIMON	Who the hell is that?
ABU DALO	My daughter. Her name is Suha. And she's from hell. You'll love her. *(takes a swig of Scotch)* Eight hundred and fifteen. Eight hundred and sixteen.
SHIMON	You never told me you had a child.
ABU DALO	I haven't told you many things. For example, I haven't told you that when I drink Scotch whisky I become incredibly intelligent; that I gain an insight into the world whereupon I see tiny white sparks lighting up the sky like a disco ball. I see the essence of things; I see the world of spirit is in fact one big disco ball.

SHIMON grabs the Scotch from ABU DALO.

SHIMON	She is not staying here.
ABU DALO	Wonderful. I didn't even invite her in. Eight hundred and seventeen. Eight hundred and eighteen. Eight hundred and nineteen.
SHIMON	Where's her mother?
ABU DALO	Dead.
SHIMON	Oh... I'm, uh—
ABU DALO	No—
SHIMON	I am—
ABU DALO	Don't say it! Don't you dare say you're sorry!
SHIMON	Well, if you need anything—
ABU DALO	I need you to shut up. My wife died. Not from old age. Not from cancer. But from a fucking bomb from your fucking army. Three lousy years ago. So leave me the hell alone. Please. *(Scratches. And wins.)* Oh

my God. I just won. I won a hundred shekels. I've never won anything before. Incredible. I feel... *(a beat)* Incredibly sad.

SHIMON   *(presents ABU DALO the cup of coffee)* Drink this.

ABU DALO   No.

SHIMON   You have a kid. Drink the coffee.

ABU DALO   No.

Flashback, 2001. Enter SHABAK AGENT.

SHABAK AGENT
        Drink it. Go on. It's good. I made it myself. *(ABU DALO refuses.)* Cigarette?

ABU DALO nods. She lights him up. They both smoke.

ABU DALO   Have you ever been to Paris?

SHABAK AGENT
        No.

ABU DALO   Are you married?

SHABAK AGENT
        Marriage gives me the creeps. Too much compromise. Who wants to fight over dirty dishes and taking out the garbage? I *like* being alone.

ABU DALO   I don't like solitude.

SHABAK AGENT
        You've been in and out of prison for nine years. You shouldn't have written the things you did. *(a beat)*

        I'm glad you came to talk. Say whatever you want. *(a beat)* Tell me about her. What colour is Yuad's hair?

| ABU DALO | My cousin Bashir. We grew up together in Ramallah. When we were kids he'd smash the heads of frogs with bricks from the construction site and laugh. |

| SHABAK AGENT | |
| | *(laughs)* That's gross. |

ABU DALO	He's disgusting and he's what's wrong with my people.
	Dr. Jihad with his four wives, all wearing hijab.
	Fourteen masked men with AK-47s by his side.
	A real religious fanatic.

| SHABAK AGENT | |
| | You have my sympathies. |

ABU DALO	I don't want your sympathy. I want him arrested.
	He organized the suicide bomb at the Tel Aviv disco.

| SHABAK AGENT | |
| | We know that, Abu Dalo. We're Shabak. |

ABU DALO	Yeah, but I know where he lives.
	Believe me, I hate you. I want a Palestinian homeland. But I can't support some fundamentalist asshole who kills children in my name. Fatah or Hamas: if we're not stealing from our own people we're blowing up innocents like those kids at the disco.

| SHABAK AGENT | |
| | I get it. |

| ABU DALO | I want to see my wife again. I want her in a new dress, on clean sheets, on a new bed, in my old house in Jerusalem. I want my house back. |

| SHABAK AGENT | |
| | We won't just arrest your cousin you know. |

| ABU DALO | I know. |

SHABAK AGENT

You'll have to do it yourself. Lure him out. Bring him to us. Dead.

ABU DALO   I know.

SHABAK AGENT

You'll have to work for us for the next five years.

ABU DALO   I know my friends in the jail are watching, I know what they are thinking. I know.

SHABAK AGENT

Drink the coffee.

Back to the present.

SHIMON   Drink it.

ABU DALO   No!

SHIMON   Take care of her. Drink the coffee.

ABU DALO   I hate your coffee. I hate your water. I hate this house. I hate everything you've touched.

SHIMON   *(A beat. ABU DALO takes the coffee but doesn't drink.)* Please. Drink my coffee. I promise to make it better next time.

            Your daughter can stay here as long as you help me finish this book.

ABU DALO   I detest your pity.

Scene 2

*Enter THE CAMEL and THE HOUSE. ALEX and SUHA digging. SUHA can hear THE HOUSE but
not ALEX. ALEX and SUHA cannot hear THE CAMEL.*

THE CAMEL sings his heart out. Leonard Cohen.

THE HOUSE   Try it with a bit more longing.

THE CAMEL	This is a complete waste of time.
THE HOUSE	I need you to sing so the kids can hear.
SUHA	The walls are full of mould. You people never took care of this place.
ALEX	You and I could clean it up. Together. If you want.
SUHA	Screw off.
THE CAMEL	This isn't helping at all.
THE HOUSE	The kids will fall in love. They'll break the impasse between the old men. They'll live like a family. They'll be a family. *(to SUHA)* Hello? Excuse me? Hello?
SUHA	Who the hell is that?
THE HOUSE	It's me. The house.

SUHA stops digging.

SUHA	Oh. You talk. I heard about a talking house once. It was in Nablus.
	The Israelis bulldozed it, of course.

SUHA AS GROUCHO
They like to bulldoze. They're like little boys with their toys in the sandbox.

SUHA resumes digging.

SUHA	They'll bulldoze you, too.
THE CAMEL	She's a real sweetheart.
THE HOUSE	Sing. *(to SUHA)* You need to stop digging.
SUHA	I'm burying my mother. *(to ALEX)* Dig, kike. *(He does.)*

ALEX	Do you like sandboxes?
SUHA	Piss off.
ALEX	I used to have a sandbox when I was a kid. Once I dug so deep I actually made it to China. *(a beat)* I'm much stronger than I look.
SUHA	You are incredibly annoying.
ALEX	You're annoyingly incredible.
SUHA	Shut up and dig!
THE CAMEL	She couldn't fall in love if you paid her.
THE HOUSE	When people disagree it means they care. Life!
	(to SUHA) This is a house for the living. Burials require special permission.
SUHA	*(to THE HOUSE)* I'm doing this because my mother wanted to be buried here. I wanted to grant her final wish.
THE HOUSE	Then it'll cost you.
SUHA	How much?
THE HOUSE	Oh, I sense a negotiation coming. I like a good negotiation.
THE CAMEL	You're beautiful when you negotiate.
THE HOUSE	Show me your hands. *(She does.)* You've got the hands of a gardener. I could do with some landscaping.
SUHA	I've never touched a plant in my life.
THE HOUSE	Then you're a cook.

SUHA	I hate cooking. I hate food. I hate boys. I hate Jews. I hate fathers. I hate trees I hate Nazis I hate soccer balls I hate high-heeled shoes I hate newspapers. I hate everything.
THE CAMEL	Not good. Not good at all.
THE HOUSE	*(to SUHA)* I know what you want.
	You want satellite television. A room of your own. A fridge full of orange Tang—
SUHA	I don't want any of that shit. Not in this house. Not with my father. He didn't even invite me inside, the prick. *(to ALEX)* Dig, kike!
ALEX	This kike is digging with zeal and determination. My pecks are glistening with sweat!
SUHA	Your pecks are small and unmanly, just like your shovel.
THE CAMEL	These kids couldn't live together if their lives depended on it. They're going to grow up to be just as messed up as their parents. Worse.
THE HOUSE	*(to SUHA)* You want to live here.
SUHA	No, I want to bury my mother.
THE HOUSE	You came to Jerusalem because you want to live in this house.
SUHA	Absolutely not. *(to ALEX)* When I'm done burying my mother I'm going right back to Jenin.
ALEX	Isn't Jerusalem nicer?
SUHA	At least I know what to expect in Jenin.
THE HOUSE	*(to THE CAMEL)* She'd rather live in a refugee camp.
THE CAMEL	She's right: you can't love here. Tragedy. That's all there is in Jerusalem. Of course, there's always Paris.

THE HOUSE	Paris.
THE CAMEL	Everything is beautiful in Paris.
THE HOUSE	A house and a camel—in Paris.
THE CAMEL	"Exiles in Paris."
THE HOUSE	You just want to sleep with me.
THE CAMEL	No, I want to make love to you. Slowly.
THE HOUSE	You don't know the first thing about love. You have to commit to love for it to work. You need to stick around. I'm not coming to Paris.
THE CAMEL	You're a fool. You wouldn't know love if it stared you right in the face.
THE HOUSE	*(to SUHA)* If you don't live here you can't bury her here.

SUHA stops digging.

SUHA	*(to THE HOUSE)* Fine. *(to ALEX)* Enough. I'm taking my mother back with me.
ALEX	But this is where your mother wanted to be.
THE HOUSE	You just said so yourself.
SUHA	I can't live here.
THE HOUSE	Sure you can. I might be falling apart but I'm no refugee camp. And a house depends on people to live in it. Not just any people. It has to be the right people—ones who don't fight and hate each other. Because otherwise a house just falls apart.
ALEX	This is where you want your mother to be.
THE HOUSE	Yuad will like it here. So will you. I promise.

THE CAMEL	Since the beginning of time:
	Neighbours, brothers, lovers, nations:
	Noise.
	That's what humans are addicted to.
	The noise stands in for life.
	Humans can't handle happiness.
	They can't handle peace.
	And they sure can't handle love.
	They don't know what to do with it.
	That's the tragedy.
	Taxi!

Scene 3

Time passes. ABU DALO, slightly more sober, typing.

SHIMON	What are you writing?
ABU DALO	*I'm* writing *your* biography. *The Story of a Nation.* And I'm using my writerly flourish.
SHIMON	We're taking the day off.
ABU DALO	Absolutely not.
SHIMON	You're not in any shape for this; you're in mourning.
ABU DALO	I want to work.
SHIMON	We can work tomorrow. Be sensible.
ABU DALO	I am sensible. I am so full of sensibility, I'm hypersensible. And my hypersensible senses are saying: I don't want to think about my dead wife.
SHIMON	*(a beat)* But I'm not telling you what to write.
ABU DALO	I know.
SHIMON	Read me what you're writing.

ABU DALO   (*still typing*) "The General's fear was his humanity: but his job demand-
                ed he keep it buried, deep within. Hidden. Even from himself."

SHIMON   What do you think you know about me?

ABU DALO   I'll read you everything when it's done.

SHIMON   I'd like to hear it now.

ABU DALO   It's not finished.

SHIMON picks up the gun.

                Put that down.

SHIMON   Read to me.

ABU DALO   No.

SHIMON   I want to know what you're writing.

ABU DALO   "The General was afraid of the enemy. But he was more afraid of
                not having an enemy. Because if he started to see the enemy as hu-
                man then he'd have to put down the gun, and without the gun he'd
                have to look at his miserable self."

SHIMON   I brought you coffee. I offered your daughter a place to live.

ABU DALO   Peace is not a fucking cup of coffee.

SHIMON   You're writing lies.

ABU DALO   No, I'm not writing lies. In fact, I'm avoiding the lies.

SHIMON   (*a beat*) You're writing your story.

ABU DALO stops typing.

ABU DALO   You know, we could finally start to talk about peace if you actu-
                ally acknowledged that I even have a story, that my family's story

in this house is possibly worth writing, that people might want to read it.

SHIMON   Are you going to publish this book?

ABU DALO resumes typing.

ABU DALO   I'm a writer. What do you think I'm going to do?

SHIMON   I negotiated with you. I let you stay here. I didn't have to.

ABU DALO   You were going to shoot me last week when I knocked on the door. You're pointing a gun at me right now.

SHIMON   I wish I'd shot you last week. I wish I'd taken care of this *problem* right then. Read to me!

ABU DALO   Why don't you just shoot me right now?

SHIMON puts down the gun.

SHIMON   That would be too easy.

ABU DALO   No, just shoot me. Come on, shoot me.

              I've had enough of this problem. Enough of *being* the problem. I've had enough of this world full of problems.

              Shoot me in the fucking eye!

SHIMON   No.

ABU DALO   Shoot me or I'll shoot myself.

ABU DALO struggles with SHIMON for the gun. ABU DALO grabs it.

              Fuck this book. Fuck this house. Fuck these four walls. Fuck my wife fuck my daughter fuck the bathroom fuck the fig tree fuck my great-grandfather. Fuck and fuck and fuck!

SHIMON	Abu Dalo, be reasonable—
ABU DALO	I tried to be reasonable. I tried to be good. But you just took advantage of me. I turned in my own cousin. An entire apartment block in Gaza went down because of me. Five years I worked for you Israelis, for your Shabak. Enough.
	When I blast this bullet through the back of my head and my brain splatters like guacamole, I hope the bullet travels to the other side through my eyes and nails you. When we're both dead, then there'll be no problem.
SHIMON	Put down the gun. You're being irrational.
ABU DALO	My wife is dead. This is a perfectly rational response. So please. Fuck off. And good riddance.

ABU DALO cocks the gun and aims it at the back of his head. He shoots. Nothing happens. Again. And again. And again. And again. And again.

	Have you been pointing an empty gun at me?
SHIMON	Yes.
ABU DALO	Why would you do that?
SHIMON	Sometimes the gun is enough.
ABU DALO	You inconsiderate asshole.
SHIMON	Abu Dalo, you're right. I do pity you. I pity your desperation. I pity your sadness. I pity your need to self-destruct.
ABU DALO	What do you want from me?
SHIMON	Read me what you wrote. Now.

Scene 4

THE CAMEL is now in Paris, smoking a cigarette and drinking café au lait.

THE CAMEL   Well friends, I'm a sneaky camel. I've done it. I made it to Paris.

I'm sure the house understands: I just needed to get away.

I get to enjoy my coffee in peace. Anonymity in a tragic and great city. The Seine at night. A little jazz. The fine derrière of a French woman. *(A waitress with a beautiful derrière walks by.)*

It occurs to me. Maybe one needs the foreign to become familiar with oneself.

Say. Look over there. That's the famous Palestinian poet Mahmoud Darwish. He looks a lot like Abu Dalo. This could be my big break.

THE CAMEL scrambles to put on a pair of Groucho Marx glasses. He grabs a microphone for the interview.

Mr. Darwish, what would it take for Israelis and Palestinians to agree to put down their arms?

Darwish ignores THE CAMEL.

(aside) Hmm. He's ignoring me. Maybe I need to ask a more original question.

If Israelis and Palestinians can't even agree on history, then what hope is there for peace?

(aside) No, too academic.

Mr. Darwish, what role do you see outsiders like camels playing in the future Middle East peace talks?

(a beat) No. Not right. Not right at all.

THE CAMEL takes off his glasses.

Mr. Darwish, can the Israeli people change? Can the Palestinians? Can anyone change—for good?

How do you get two people who hate each other to live in the same house?

Is love important in any of this?

MAHMOUD DARWISH
    Love? I don't want to talk about it. I only want to make it.

He snaps his fingers and leaves with the waitress with the beautiful derrière.

Scene 5

SUHA   The House is right. If I'm going to bury her here, I have to live here.

ALEX   Of course you can live here. I'll move out of my room. I'll sleep on the couch.

SUHA   But I can't live with him. And I can't live with you, Moses.

ALEX   Why not? I could be a Jew. I could be Muslim. Part goat. Part camel. I could be your sister. The great thing is nobody knows who I am. Not even me.

    I'm loyal to no one. I have to be good to everyone. I have to save the entire Middle East or else risk complete purposelessness.

SUHA   Right.

    Do you hate your father?

ALEX   Absolutely.

SUHA   Why?

ALEX   Because nothing he says is true. Do you hate your father?

SUHA   Hatred is too soft a word for what I feel about the man who donated his sperm to my mother.

SUHA AS GROUCHO

    Fathers are like matzo balls.

    By the time you're finished your soup they're gone.

ALEX AS GROUCHO

    What was it like to have a mother?

SUHA   My mother was screwed up. She used to boil an egg for so long the shell would split and the egg white would get all stringy in the water.

SUHA AS GROUCHO

    She liked to watch things break.

ALEX   Oh.

SUHA   When there was a curfew, and the fighting would get so loud you didn't know who was shooting who, when and if the door would break in, and who would live and who would die, we used to lie together on her bed. She'd hold me. And sing.

ALEX   And then what?

SUHA   Isn't that enough?

ALEX   What did that do?

SUHA   It made me feel that even though I could die at any second, in that moment everything was all right. And that's all we have. That moment.

ALEX   Well I could hold you.

SUHA   Why would you do that?

ALEX   Because nobody else will.

SUHA   But I don't like you.

ALEX   Yeah, but you're upset.

SUHA	I'm not upset. I'm just about to bury my mother.
ALEX	That means you're upset.
SUHA	Shut up. You have no idea what I'm talking about. You never had a mother and your father never abandoned you.
	(a beat) Shit. What are we doing here? Why are you helping me? My father's supposed to be here. Where the hell is he now? Why the hell was he never around?
ALEX	Are you trying to say I've never felt like shit?
SUHA	What?
ALEX	Yes you are. You're totally saying that I've never felt like shit.
SUHA	No I'm not.
ALEX	Well of course I've felt like shit. My whole life I've felt like shit. You had a mother at least. I'm sorry she blew up, but you have memories of her. You did things together. I don't even have that. I have nothing.
	Everything I do is to try and escape the shit that life is, this screwed-up "situation." When I say I want to hold you, it's because I'm hoping maybe you in my arms could be something different. Maybe there is a world that isn't full of shit.
SUHA	That's an interesting thought.
ALEX	Yeah well there you go. I'm an interesting human being.
SUHA	But I really don't want you to hold me.
ALEX	Fine.
SUHA	No offence. We just met.
ALEX	I get it.

SUHA	I mean, my mother was the one who did that, and we're going to bury her. And I can't just replace her, you know? *(a beat)*
	Maybe you could do something else instead.
	You could do your thing.
ALEX	My what?
SUHA	Do your thing.
ALEX	Down here?
SUHA	Yeah. Why not?
ALEX	But you have cataplexy.
SUHA	I know.
ALEX	If I give you cunnilingus, you could faint. If you faint, you could go unconscious. If you go unconscious, you could die.
SUHA	So.
ALEX	You want to die with me giving you cunnilingus on your mother's grave?
SUHA	No, I don't want to die. I want to beat death. I want to say, death, get lost. I want to say, give me life. Give me now. Give me you.

She moves toward ALEX. Kisses him abruptly, briefly.

ALEX	Ouch.
SUHA	I don't know why I did that.
ALEX	My cheek is burning.
SUHA	I wasn't thinking.

ALEX	That's cool. I'd like to not think. To feel something. I'd like that. To feel.

She starts to laugh. She stops herself.

	That wasn't meant to be funny.
SUHA	I know.
ALEX	How are we going to do this? I can't even unintentionally make you laugh.
SUHA	Go slow. So how do we start?
ALEX	I don't know. I've never done this before.
SUHA	I thought you were some kind of expert.
ALEX	I have done extensive research.
SUHA	So you're a scientist. You've got theories and now you have to put them into practise.
ALEX	You're going to have to take off your pants.
SUHA	Turn off your flashlight. *(Flashlights turned off. Slowly she undresses.)*

ALEX aside.

ALEX	Houston, I'm in the cockpit.
HOUSTON	Copy, Alex. Rockets. Lights. All systems go. Ready to commence countdown.
ALEX	Uhm, I'm a bit nervous.
HOUSTON	Copy, Alex. The entire Middle East is counting on you, Ilan Ramon's counting on you.

COUNTING VOICE
10-9-8-

| SUHA | Whoah. |

| COUNTING VOICE | |
| | 7-6-5- |

| SUHA | Hold on. |

| COUNTING VOICE | |
| | 4-3-2- |

| SUHA | You're not a rocket ship. |

| ALEX | I'm about to travel to the mysterious cosmos. To the unknown of Palestine and Woman. To you. So much depends on this moment. On what I do to you. On us. |

| SUHA | Nothing depends on us, idiot. I just want to try this out. |

ALEX fumbles around.

| ALEX | Do you know where your clitoris is? |

| SUHA | What's that? |

| ALEX | It's a part of your body that exists only for the sake of sexual pleasure. |

| SUHA | Seriously? |

| ALEX | Yes. It's very sensitive. It has like sixty-eight thousand different nerve endings. They say it's the best way to please a woman. I read that in *Cosmo*. |

| SUHA | I hate *Cosmo*. |

| ALEX | It's got good pictures. And maps. It's very helpful. There's this big controversy about the g-spot. People can't decide whether or not it exists. |

| SUHA | People are idiots. |

ALEX	You're beautiful.
SUHA	You can't see me.
ALEX	I like talking to you.
SUHA	No you don't. Don't you dare say that.
ALEX	Yeah. I do. And I like it when you talk to me.
SUHA	You're lying.
ALEX	I'm telling the truth.
	I'm speaking to you. And now I'm touching. You.
SUHA	I feel like I'm about to melt into a puddle of water.
ALEX	I think I found the clitoris.

SUHA gasps, almost passes out.

	You're not going to die, are you?
SUHA	No.
	There's a slight burning in my head.
ALEX	That's normal when you leave the stratosphere.

Scene 6

Paris. THE CAMEL reading Le Monde.

THE CAMEL	Suha has an orgasm whose effects are felt right across the Middle East.

In the Negev, nuclear missiles in their bunkers sigh.
In Bethlehem, the wall cracks a smile.
And in Tel Aviv a frustrated theatre director drops his gun before he's about to shoot himself in the head.

The effect of the orgasm does not stop there.
In Baghdad two people make love in the back of a bombed-out mosque.
Osama bin Laden has a dream he's playing table tennis with Halle
Berry and winning.

There are all sorts of effects. Even the stratosphere heats up. This is
something Alex could not have anticipated.

The stratosphere heats up. And at that very moment, the space shuttle *Columbia* re-enters the earth's atmosphere. It catches fire, blows up
into a thousand and one pieces over Palestine, Texas.

Smack. Damned. Boom.

Ilan Ramon. The hope of a nation. Dead.

Scene 7

ABU DALO   "1988. Things were quiet—
the occupation of the West Bank continued its gentle course of
normalcy,
over twenty years in.
But the General didn't trust the silence. It was too quiet.
He could see it in the eyes of the occupied,
the Palestinians he passed on his way to the military base on the hill
overlooking everything.
They were tired, scared.
Fear, he knows, eventually can turn.

The General liked to drive the highway from the Dead Sea to Jericho,
alongside the Jordan River.
He would drive it, thinking, this is the road of our forefathers.
Joshua the warrior,
Abraham the father,
Ecclesiastes the prophet.
How beautiful, he thought,
to return to this country.
Inheritance.

It was hot out that day.
You could see the heat rising above the highway outside Jericho.

The General left his army Jeep at home—he took the car,
the top down, sun baking his head.
The radio played "Hatikvah," "The Hope."
The General had chills in heat.

At a checkpoint near the Jordan River,
five bearded men kneeling in a line by the side of the road.
Their hands were over their heads; they'd been holding them up like
this for hours.
ID cards on the ground.
He saw his soldiers laughing, smoking in the sun.
"We're taking them in," said the corporal. "Questioning."

One of them was Zayid.
Zayid looked familiar, though the General wasn't sure where he'd seen
him before.
Was he the neighbour at the kibbutz, the one he'd waved to as a young
man?
Was he the falafel man, the one in the Arab village he sometimes
stopped at on the way to work?
He couldn't remember. Nothing was clear in that heat.

The General pointed to him and said,

SHIMON   "You. Go home now."

ABU DALO   But Zayid wouldn't move.

SHIMON   "You can go home,"

ABU DALO   said the General.

           Zayid wouldn't speak.

SHIMON   "Go on. It's okay."

ABU DALO   The others were looking at him, trying to get his attention, eyeing
           him, go on, get out, run while you can.

SHIMON   "Here,"

ABU DALO   the General said, and brought Zayid a canteen of water.

SHIMON   "Drink this. You're thirsty."

ABU DALO   The General wasn't aware of what he was doing, why he was doing it.
Perhaps he felt an unconscious need for compassion;
the habit to feed those who are thirsty.

Zayid wouldn't drink; he smiled at the General; they were both drunk from the sun.

SHIMON   "I'm offering you this. You need it. Drink."

ABU DALO   Zayid said something in Arabic. Unintelligible. He told the General to fuck off, fuck his mother, to lay his head down in the shit box he belonged in.

SHIMON   "I'm offering you water."

ABU DALO   Zayid still wouldn't take it.

SHIMON   "I'm offering you life!"

ABU DALO   Zayid took the canteen, drank a mouthful, then spit in the General's face.

Now the General drew his gun.

SHIMON   "Take the water!"

ABU DALO   The General weighs the pistol in his hand. And the soldiers are wondering, what the hell is he doing? The guy won't drink the water, surely there's nothing wrong with that.

SHIMON   "Take it!"

ABU DALO   And the General hits Zayid on the cheek with the back of the Mauser.

SHIMON   "Enough!"

ABU DALO	Cried the General and he hits him again. Zayid's face a river of blood—
SHIMON	"Enough!"
ABU DALO	And the General hits the Arab's face one last time.
SHIMON	"Enough..."

SHIMON (cont.)

And when Zayid's breathing stops, I look up at the horizon.

And I can no longer read the signs on the highway that point to the cities of my forefathers. A strange and sudden blindness of words.

Scene 8

Lights up on SHIMON *and* ABU DALO. SHIMON *is blind.*

ABU DALO	Your son brought me the ammo box hidden beneath your floorboards. I was happy for the first time in my life. Happiness is vengeance. I wrote your story. I will publish it, I will destroy you with words. You'll be disgraced in front of the entire world, and I will take back this house—I'll take back what's mine.

Your own son had to betray you. To me. A Palestinian.

Enter ALEX *and* SUHA.

ALEX	Dad, Mr. Abu Dalo— I have seen the truth! In the hills of Jerusalem, a great and wondrous miracle has happened!

SUHA *starts to laugh.*

SUHA	That's the jut-jut laugh. The chihuahua. The dagger. The holly-hoo.
ALEX	Yes! She doesn't have cataplexy anymore. She's cured. It's the Miracle of Cunnilingus.

Know that the cunnilingus revolution has brought peace to the Middle East! Witness that we have been led from darkness and war to a world of harmony and great cosmic desire!

SUHA   You and I are getting married.

ALEX   Wow. I'm totally speechless.

ABU DALO   You think this is Romeo and fucking Juliet? You're not getting married.

SUHA   Sure we are. We have to get married. I have to live here. You have to live here. Our fathers have to live here. My dead mother—she's going to live here too. We're going to be like a family. We will be a family. I assume this is my father-in-law. Pleased to meet you, Daddy.

ABU DALO   No daddy. No way. *(to SHIMON)* Admit to your future daughter-in-law what you did. Tell your son's fiancée what kind of family she wants to marry into. That her husband-to-be is the son of a murderer of her people.

SHIMON   *(to ABU DALO)* You don't know the whole story.

SUHA   I don't care about that story. *(to SHIMON)* Call a fumigator. I want the basement cleaned. I want this room clean. *(to ALEX)* Can you cook?

ALEX   I can boil an egg.

SUHA   We can learn how to cook. We'll learn everything. How to take care of things. We have to.

ABU DALO   *(to SUHA)* I won't let you become one of them. You cannot forget who you are. You're Jenin. You're your mother. You're this house—thirty-five years ago. I won't let you forget, he won't let you forget, no one in this country will let you forget, because an Israeli cannot marry a Palestinian, a Palestinian cannot marry an Israeli—by history, by lineage, by law. End of story.

THE HOUSE   I'll marry them.

ABU DALO   Shut up and stay out of this.

THE HOUSE	I want these two to marry. I want love. Love to destroy history.
ALEX	Whoah, citizens of Jerusalem, the miracle of the Cunnilingus Revolution is confirmed! The house speaketh! *(He bows.)* The house will marry us.
THE HOUSE	Do you, Alex, son of Shimon, and Suha, daughter of Abu Dalo, promise to love and care for me, to feed my garden water and fertilizer, to put in a decent television with cable, to make goofy home videos of your children, to plant a fig tree—
SUHA & ALEX	We do.
ABU DALO	Oh no you don't.
SUHA	Oh yes I do.
ABU DALO	You know nothing about love.
SUHA	Sure I do.
ALEX	We spoke to each other. She listened. That's pretty amazing. Nobody's ever listened to me before. And Dad, I never listened.
SHIMON	You can't know love, kid. Not in this house.
ABU DALO	They're fifteen. *(to SUHA)* You only want sex.
SUHA	Don't start talking to me like a father. Where were you? When I started to walk. When they closed the schools down. When the gunfire was so loud I couldn't sleep at night—
ABU DALO	In jail. For fifteen years, I rotted in jail. Your mother knew.
SUHA	We had no idea where you were.
SHIMON	Tell her the truth, Abu Dalo. And I'll tell them mine. Let's see if they can live with it.

ABU DALO	Absolutely not! I did nothing a father wouldn't do. I thought only of you and this house. You do not love this Jew. You cannot love him.
SUHA	This is love. It's a way of talking.
ABU DALO	Talking. Right. Tell me, Groucho. What do you have to say about this kike? These Chosen People who've chosen to take our land? To kill our wives and mothers?

Groucho can't talk.

SHIMON	*(a beat)* Sarah and I lived in this house.
	It was beautiful.
	Everything's beautiful when you're young.
	We had a garden.
	She worked at the school.
	You were small as a peanut.
	The army reports don't mention that, do they?
	Don't mention I loved your mother either.
	I took the car to work that day.
	She left you in the house.
	She was going to bring the Jeep closer so she wouldn't have to carry you so far. You were getting so big.
	I was in the car driving the Dead Sea highway. The West Bank.
	The sun beat down on my head.
	It was hot.
	They called me on the radio; I answered it.
	They gave me the news:
	She turned on the ignition.
	The Jeep blew up.
	Her body scattered everywhere.
	I was sure you were in there too.
	Nothing made sense in that heat.
	I pulled over and tried to give Zayid water. But he wouldn't take it.

ALEX	You fucker. Why didn't you tell me?
SHIMON	I didn't want you to have to bury her.

Scene 9

Sound of rain. Time passes. The sound of water dripping into a bucket gets louder through the scene. SHIMON and ALEX on one side of THE HOUSE, ABU DALO and SUHA on the other. ABU DALO smoking, hammering, SUHA passing him nails. SHIMON and ALEX carry cinder blocks to the centre of the stage.

Lights up on THE CAMEL and THE HOUSE.

THE CAMEL   So what's going to happen next?

THE HOUSE   Shimon's building a wall. He's trying to occupy more than half the house.

THE CAMEL   I hear Abu Dalo's building an extension.

THE HOUSE   He's not so good with his hands.

THE CAMEL   Don't be sad. You got what you wanted, right? Life.

THE HOUSE   Some life this is. Winter in Jerusalem. My roof's leaking and no one's bothering to fix it. Nobody's taking care of me.

Why does history make life so difficult?

THE CAMEL   Life is difficult no matter where you are.

Say. I brought you some French cigarettes. They make you absolutely sexy. Guaranteed. *(Hands her a smoke. Lights her up.)* See? You're brighter already.

THE HOUSE   You were right. This is a tragedy. But you came back.

THE CAMEL   The problem with leaving is you never really go. Not completely, at least.

THE HOUSE   My problem is I can't really let go of things. I hold on too tight: to people, ideas, land, love.

THE CAMEL   Holding on means you have hope. There's nothing wrong with that.

THE HOUSE   I'm starting to think there is. Hope makes compromise very difficult. I mean, who wants to compromise when there's something better around the corner?

THE CAMEL   You know, I really missed you.

THE HOUSE   Yeah? Would you make me a promise?

A beat.

THE CAMEL   Absolutely not.

ABU DALO puts down his hammer and starts carrying cinder blocks. The wall takes shape. ALEX and SUHA approach the wall separating the two sides of THE HOUSE. They touch their respective sides and listen.

The end.

Acknowledgements

Thanks to:

Gadi Roll and John Murrell for initial insights and dramaturgy.
The Banff Playwrights Colony for the original workshop and time to write.
Maureen Labonté.
Daryl Cloran and all previous workshop actors.
Thanks to Lise Anne Johnson and On the Verge Festival.
Akademie Schloss Solitude.
Frank Heibert for translation, edits and understanding.
Bastian Haefner, my man in Berlin, and Michael Petrasek, in Toronto.
ITI and the Maxim Gorki Theatre in Berlin.
Kristo Šagor, Holger Weimar and Bochum Schauspielhaus for the wild and loose production.
Jonathan Chadwick for the London variation. And Caryne Chapman Clark for setting that up.
Richard Rose, Andrea Romaldi, Camilla Holland and the Tarragon Theatre for the workshops, the commitment and the final deal.
Adam Sol, Udi Avnery, Martha Schabas, Marni Jackson, Medeine Tribinevicius and Manfred Becker for their careful readings of the text.
Bobby Theodore for his "good bad jokes."
Eric Woodley for his usual magic throughout.
Finally, thanks to friends in Palestine and Israel, including Suha Diab, Samer Shalabi, Eytan Bronstein and Heidi Levine. Your insights were invaluable.

Jonathan Garfinkel has written a book of poetry, *Glass Psalms* (Turnstone Press), and the book *Ambivalence: Crossing the Israel/Palestine Divide* (published in Canada, US, UK, Germany and Hungary). His play *The Trials of John Demjanjuk: A Holocaust Cabaret* has been performed in Canada and Germany and was published by Playwrights Canada Press. *House of Many Tongues* was produced at the Bochum Schauspielhaus in Germany, and then at the Tarragon Theatre in Toronto. His articles have appeared in the *Globe and Mail*, *Pen International*, *Judische Allgemeine* and the *Walrus*. Jonathan divides his time between Berlin and Toronto.